Little book of
Kittens

BBC

Little Book of Kittens

First published in 1999
by BBC Worldwide Ltd
80 Wood Lane, London W12 0TT

ISBN 0 563 55601 3

Text, specially-commissioned photography,
illustrations and design
copyright © BBC Worldwide Ltd 1999

RSPCA name and logo are trademarks of the
RSPCA licensed by RSPCA Trading Ltd
RSPCA is a registered charity no. 219099

Animal Hospital is a trademark of the BBC
Animal Hospital logo copyright © BBC

Colour Reproduction by
Dot Gradations Limited, Wickford
Printed and bound in Italy

Contents

- 6 Think Before You Get A Kitten
- 8 True Story: Water Baby
- 10 A-Z Of Kitten Names
- 12 Make It! Kitten Place Cards
- 14 Having Kittens
- 16 True Story: The Mitcham Kittens
- 18 10 Ways To Love Your Kitten
- 20 Welcome Home Kitten
- 22 Pedigree Cats
- 24 The Kitten Kit
- 26 True Story: Trouble
- 28 Stay Flea Free!
- 30 Make It! Kitten Playhouse
- 32 Around The Home
- 34 Record-Breaking Kitties
- 36 Training Your Kitten
- 38 Kitten's Diet
- 41 True Story: Fallout
- 44 10 Show Names
- 46 Is My Kitten Ill?
- 48 Kittens In The Wild
- 50 True Story: Sam's Sneezes
- 52 Kitten Loves And Pet Hates
- 56 When To Call The Vet
- 58 True Story: Snoring Kitten
- 60 Kitten Party Recipes
- 62 Sleep
- 64 Cat And Kitten Facts
- 66 True Story: Up To Scratch
- 68 Paws And Claws
- 70 Make It! Scratching Post
- 72 All About Fur
- 74 True Story: Up On The Roof
- 76 10 Kitten Toys
- 78 Make It! Catnip Toy
- 80 As Your Kitten Grows
- 82 How Your Kitten Talks
- 86 House Moves And Holidays
- 88 We Love Kittens
- 90 True Story: Tom's Tum
- 92 You And Your Kitten
- 96 Tips For Kits!

THINK

A cat is a wonderful pet but owning one is a great responsibility. The first few months of a kitten's life are particularly important. Its early experiences will shape both the mental and physical health of the adult cat. Here are some questions to ask yourself before you consider owning a cat:

- Are you prepared to commit yourself to looking after a kitten for the whole of its life?
- Do you have the time and patience needed to train your kitten?
- Will you ensure that your kitten receives a balanced diet?
- Are you able to give your kitten enough physical and mental exercise?
- Are you prepared to be responsible for

BEFORE YOU GET A KITTEN

your kitten's healthcare, including vaccinations, worming, dental care and grooming?
- Can you afford the expense of a kitten's food, equipment and healthcare, especially if it gets sick and needs treatment from a vet?
- Who will take care of your kitten when you go on holiday? Or can you afford to put it in a cattery?
- What sort of kitten will suit you? Pedigree kittens are expensive. 'Moggies' and cross-breeds are cheaper but you will know less about its likely traits.
- Would you prefer a male or female kitten?
- Where will you get your kitten from? Getting your kitten from an animal rescue centre or asking a local vet, friend or neighbour you trust is often better than looking in a pet shop or answering an advert.
- Do you have any other pets? How will they react to your kitten? Can you see any potential problems?
- What about the rest of your family? Remember that the adults must be in overall charge of any pets. They will need to ensure your pet gets the best care.

TRUE STORY — Water

Cruelty to tiny defenceless animals is something that is all too often faced by the RSPCA.

In this incident, a kitten of about seven weeks old was found by an RSPCA officer in a toilet with the lid down. The kitten's head was just out of the water.

RSPCA staff had no idea how long the kitten had been there, but he was visibly exhausted and terrified. Apart from being wet, the RSPCA inspector thought the kitten looked quite well but he wanted to be sure. He took the kitten to RSPCA Harmsworth Animal Hospital to be checked by a veterinary surgeon.

The vet checked for breathing problems and signs of water on the lungs. Apart from shock and hunger, the poor kitten was unhurt and he was soon snapped up by a loving new owner.

A to Z of

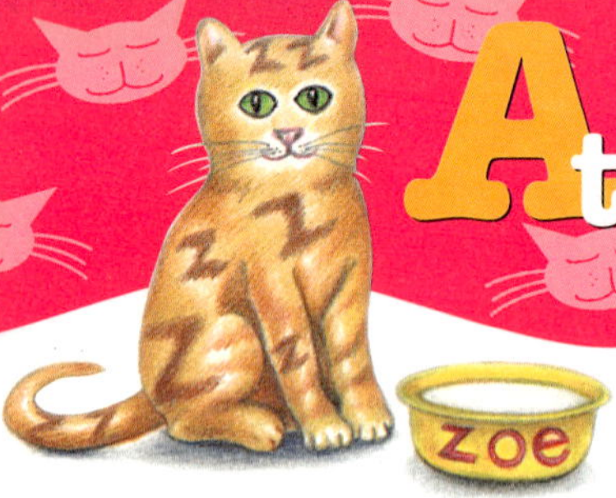

Having trouble naming your kitten? Then have a look at some of our favourites!

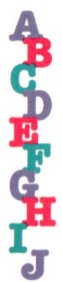

A Alfie, Angel, Atom, Arthur
B Bluey, Biscuit, Bella, Boris
C Cuddles, Casper, Crumble, Cleo
D Dolly, Doodle, Dandy, Dudley
E Ellie, Ernie, Emerald, Elvis
F Felix, Fliss, Fire, Finnie
G Ginger, Goldie, Giddie, Grumble
H Harvey, Hazel, Hamish, Harley
I Indie, Ivy, Izzy, Ice-cream
J Jester, Junior, Jarvis, Jumble

Kitten Names

K Katie, Kitkat, Kiss, Ketchup
L Leo, Lavender, Liquorice, Lilac
M Muffin, Millie, Mungo, Monster
N Ned, Nicknack, Nibble, Nougat
O Othello, Ollie, Otto, Orchid
P Peanut, Paris, Poppy, Percy
Q Queenie, Quentin, Quicksilver, Quaver
R Rupert, Rhubarb, Rollo, Rocket
S Snowy, Sardine, Smoky, Scruff
T Tabitha, Teddy, Tiger, Thimble
U Ulrika, Urchin, Ursula, Umber
V Velvet, Vinnie, Violet, Victor
W Whitesock, Win, Wellington, Wafer
X Xanadu, Xanthe, Xavier, X-ray
Y Yasmin, Yuri, Yippee, Yo-yo
Z Zoe, Zigzag, Zero, Zebedee

MAKE IT!

Kitten Name

Did you know that kittens shouldn't eat sweets? Well, it doesn't mean their owners have to miss out! Try making these sweet-filled place cards. You can use them at a kitten-themed party to wow your friends with your purrr...fect kitten recipes (see pages 60 and 61 for ideas)!

YOU WILL NEED:
- Coloured card
- Felt-tip pens
- Scissors
- Strong glue
- Glitter
- Sweets

1. Fold an A4 size sheet of coloured card in half.
2. Draw the outline of a kitten on one half of the

Cards

card, making sure the bottom of your picture meets up with the folded edge.

3. Unfold the card and cut out the shape leaving the bottom edge attached to the other half of your card.
4. Write your guest's name on the kitten's tummy.
5. Add the details such as eyes and whiskers, using felt-tip pens.
6. Put a thin layer of glue over the name and then sprinkle with glitter.
7. Shake off any excess glitter and leave to dry.
8. Cut a strip of card about 3cm wide and 20cm long.
9. Curve it into a semi-circle and, using glue, fix it to the back of the cat, resting on the other side of the card. You now have a base.
10. Cut off all the excess card on your base to leave you with a tray for the sweets.
11. Fill the tray with your favourite sweets. This gives the place card weight and helps it stand up properly.

HAVING KI...

CHOOSING YOUR KITTEN

Always inspect a kitten's state of health and condition. Look for a kitten which is friendly, alert, playful and willing to be handled. There are a number of things to look out for, but remember that the kitten will probably be nervous at being handled by a complete stranger. Try playing with the kitten a little to put it at ease. Then hold the kitten's

body firmly but gently to prevent it from escaping. Don't forget to take it slowly! Any sudden movement may alarm the kitten.

CHECK IT OUT

COAT The kitten's fur should be smooth and unmatted. Check the fur for fleas (see pages 28 and 29).
EYES AND NOSE Its eyes should be clean and bright and its nose should be damp.
EARS The kitten's ears should be clean and dry. Make sure they aren't filled with red-brown wax.
MOUTH AND TEETH A healthy kitten has a pink mouth and white teeth. Check that its gums aren't swollen.
BOTTOM The kitten's bottom should be clean and not sore.

TRUE STORY

The Mitcham

The problems faced by pet owners are not always straightforward. Take the Mitcham kittens, for example.

During the birth of her five kittens, the mother had to have emergency surgery which meant she was unable to look after her newborn kittens. The RSPCA were called because the cat's owner couldn't cope with the enormous task of hand-rearing all five kittens. Although the owner wanted to help and was reluctant to give up the kittens, she knew it would be best for them to go somewhere where they could be properly looked after.

The RSPCA officer took the kittens, which were only days old, to the veterinary surgeon in Putney. The vet explained that it is not just feeding day and night that the mother is needed for, but that by licking her kittens, the mother stimulates blood circulation and encourages the kittens to go to the toilet.

Kittens

Nurses at the RSPCA Animal Hospital used syringes to feed the kittens a special milk substitute and then used damp cotton wool to simulate a licking action to make them go to the toilet.

So what next? Once the kitten's health improved, the RSPCA set about finding them new homes.

WAYS TO LOVE YOUR KITTEN

1. Give your kitten its favourite treat if it is raining and windy outside.
2. Sit your kitten on your lap and stroke it under its chin and behind its ears.
3. Grow some of your kitten's favourite plants in the garden and indoors (see page 52).
4. If it is a cold night, put a warm hot water bottle, wrapped in a blanket, inside your kitten's bed.
5. Play some games with your kitten every day.
6. When you groom your kitten, rub in some bay rum conditioner and then brush it out to give body and shine to its coat.
7. Keep your kitten inside on Bonfire Night.
8. Wash your kitten's bedding regularly.
9. Worm your kitten regularly and check its mouth for swollen gums and its coat for fleas and pests.
10. Always take note of your kitten's behaviour for signs of illness.

WELCOME HO

The first time you bring your kitten home, it is likely to be frightened and confused. You can help to put it at ease by following our 10 tips to welcoming your kitten home for the first time.

1. Make sure you provide essential kitten equipment (see pages 24 and 25). Put the kitten's bed in a warm, quiet place.
2. Have some food and water already laid out for your kitten on its arrival.
3. Talk quietly to your kitten to let it get used to the sound of your voice.
4. Open the pet carrier and let your kitten look

ME KITTEN

around. Encourage (but do not force) your kitten to come out.

5. Let the kitten explore its surroundings, showing it one room at a time and where you've put its food, water, tray and bed.

6. Keep other pets and small children away from the new kitten until it has had time to adjust, then supervise the initial encounters.

7. Let your kitten explore you. It will want to smell you and may rub itself up against you.

8. Introduce yourself! Crouch down and stay very still. Hold out your hand so that your kitten can sniff your fingers. If it is nervous this may take some time.

9. Stroke your kitten by smoothing down its fur gently in the direction that it grows. Stroke it around its ears and under its chin. Most cats don't like their tummy being touched.

10. Be patient; move slowly and quietly. Allow your kitten time to settle in at its own pace.

PEDIGR

There are over 100 different recognised breeds and colour varieties of pedigree domestic cat.
Breeds can be divided into five basic categories:
1. Persians
2. Other long-haired cats
3. British shorthairs
4. American shorthairs
5. Foreign shorthairs

Here are the 10 most popular breeds of kitten registered by the Governing Council of the Cat Fancy, GCCF:
1. Persian Long Hair
2. Siamese
3. British Short Hair
4. Burmese

Nine-week-old Burmese kitten

EE CATS

5. Birman
6. Oriental Short Hair
7. Maine Coon
8. Bengal
9. Ragdoll
10. Exotic Short Hair

While pedigree cats and kittens are very popular, many, particularly Siamese and Persians, are also popular with thieves. This is because they can be valuable. Make sure you get your kitten microchipped (see page 97).

You should also consider the fact that pedigree cats have quite distinctive characters and, if you do choose a pedigree, make sure you choose one with a temperament that will suit yours.

Moreover, long-haired cats need daily grooming. So think carefully before you consider getting a long-haired pedigree kitten.

The Kitten

Although there is a wide range of equipment available for a kitten, few items are essential. Of the selection of items listed below, only the following items are vital: Cat bed, litter tray and scoop, carrier, food and water dishes and grooming tools. Other items can be bought or made later if you feel they are necessary.

- **Carrying basket**
- **Cat bed**
- **Scratching post**
- **Cat toys**
- **Litter tray and scoop**
- **Cat flap**
- **Food and water dishes**
- **Wire/bristle brush**

Kit

- Fine/wide-toothed comb
- Rubber brush
- Play pen
- Cat collar with elastic insert and name tag

TRUE STORY: Trouble

'Trouble' is a little black kitten who lived up to her name. One Christmas, she went crazy for decorations: fairy lights, tinsel, baubles on the tree and even the little bows on presents were not safe when Trouble was around!

When Trouble's owner brought the kitten into the RSPCA Animal Hospital, she explained how Trouble had gone into the lounge and scaled the Christmas tree, only to fall off onto a nearby sideboard.

Trouble's owner had heard her cries and saw that the kitten couldn't move properly. Trouble was in pain.

The veterinary surgeon examined Trouble and saw that the back left paw was very painful. She thought the problem might be caused by Trouble's knee but wanted to check her hip as well.

This was going to need an x-ray, but Trouble didn't seem too keen on that idea. Even anaesthetising Trouble was a three-person job, but once Trouble wa

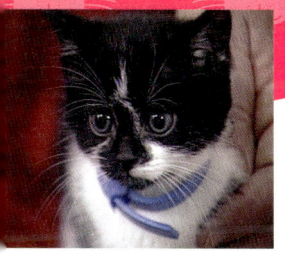

sound asleep, the vet could get to work.

The vet saw that Trouble's left hip was badly broken. Although an operation would be able to fix this, Trouble was too tiny and the operation would be too tricky and risky for the kitten. The vet decided the best thing to do would be to strap up Trouble's hip and, with plenty of rest, the hip might mend itself.

She explained to Trouble's owner that Trouble would need rest. She should be kept indoors and, most importantly, out of mischief!

Keeping Trouble out of trouble was going to be a full-time job!

STAY FLEA

FLEAS!

Even the best cared for and most loved kitten will probably get fleas from time to time.

Fleas are red-brown, wingless, jumping insects. They are easily visible to the naked eye but can run around fairly fast through a kitten's fur.

Adult fleas feed by sucking an animal's blood and can cause a kitten to scratch and bite itself. More serious is that some kittens may become allergic or hypersensitive to flea bites. In such cases, even a few bites can provoke a severe irritation, leading to hair loss, self-mutilation and thickening of the skin. Allergic kittens should be taken straight to the vet.

HOW TO SPOT A FLEA

Even mild flea infestations can be spotted easily. While it is not always easy to spot an individual flea, it is usually easy to find flea droppings in a kitten's coat.

Flea droppings look like black specks or 'coal dust' powder. To check for this, put a damp piece of white

FREE!

kitchen roll underneath the kitten and rub its fur briskly with your fingers. Any flea dirt falling on to the wet towel will quickly dissolve to show a dark red smudge (a bloodstained circle spreading outwards).

Ask a vet for advice on how best to treat your kitten and your home for fleas.

● KITTEN TIP

When checking your kitten for fleas and flea dirt, part the fur so that you can look right down onto the skin. Pay special attention to the area down the centre of the back and towards the base of the tail. And always check closely where the kitten has been scratching – your kitten knows best!

MAKE IT!

Kitten

Kittens love to play. They like climbing inside boxes and paper bags. They are also very inquisitive and enjoy exploring new things. Encouraging your kitten to play makes exercise fun. So why not follow our Make It! steps to making a playhouse. Good luck!

YOU WILL NEED:
- Large cardboard box
- Scissors or knife
- Paint for decoration
- Sticky tape
- Piece of thick A3 paper or light card

Playhouse

1. Find a large cardboard box which has four flaps at the top.
2. Bend the flaps out of the box and draw a circle on one flap.
3. Draw circles of varying sizes on all sides of the box, apart from the base!
4. Get an adult to help you carefully cut out the circles with a sharp knife or scissors.
5. Make a tunnel by joining the short ends of the A3 paper with sticky tape.
6. Snip one end of the tunnel in six places to make small flaps.
7. Bend out the paper flaps and stick them over a large circle using sticky tape.
8. Firmly stick down the flaps of the box with the tape.
9. Paint the playhouse with bright colours and jazz it up with painted hearts, paw prints, fish shapes or mice for extra fun!

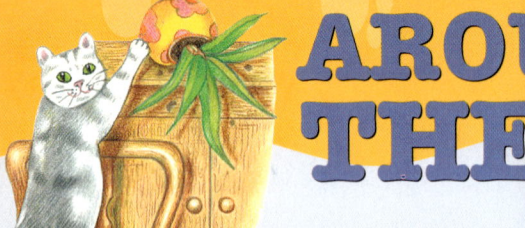

AROU
THE

Even though you may think your house quite safe, the inquisitive nature of kittens can lead them into trouble. Thinking of a kitten in terms of a small child helps you to spot potential hazards.

- Don't leave sharp utensils out!
- Don't leave toxic household products in accessible places!
- Put valued ornaments out of your kitten's reach!
- Don't leave small objects where your kitten may swallow or step on them!
- Make sure all rubbish is hidden from your kitten!
- Don't let your kitten chew on electricity cables!

ND HOME

- Install a safety guard around open fires!
- Don't let your kitten walk on kitchen surfaces, especially the cooker!
- Make sure the plants you keep indoors and in your garden are not poisonous!

CHECKLIST
Plants which are poisonous to cats include:
- Mistletoe
- Rhododendron (Azalea)
- Oleander
- True Ivy
- Poinsettia
- False Jerusalem Cherry
- Common or cherry laurel

RECORD BRE...

FATTEST CAT
The heaviest recorded cat was called Himmy. It weighed 21.3kg when it died on March 12, 1986, aged ten years.

SMALLEST CAT
Tinker Toy, a male blue point Himalayan-Persian cat who lives in Illinois, USA, is just 7cm tall and 19cm long.

OLDEST CAT
The oldest reliably recorded cat was a female tabby called Ma. Ma was put down on November 5, 1957, aged 34.

MOST PROLIFIC CAT
A tabby from Texas, USA, called Dusty produced 420 kittens. She gave birth to her last litter on June 12, 1952.

LARGEST LITTER
A Burmese/Siamese cat from Oxfordshire gave birth to the largest litter on August 7, 1970. She had 19 kittens, of whom four were stillborn.

OLDEST CAT MOTHER
In May 1987, a 30-year-old cat called Litty had two kittens.

BEST CLIMBER
A four-month-old kitten from Geneva in Switzerland followed climbers to the summit of Matterhorn (4,478m) on September 6, 1950.

KING KITTIES

EARLIEST CAT TO HAVE A NAME
The first cat recorded as having a name was Nedjem (which means 'sweet' or 'pleasant'), who lived during the reign of the Egyptian pharoah Thutmose III (1479BC to 1425BC).

MOST TRAVELLED CAT
Hamlet escaped from his cage on a flight from Toronto, Canada, and travelled 965,600km (600,000 miles) in just over seven weeks, until he was caught in February 1984.

RICHEST CAT
Blackie was left £15million in the will of his millionaire owner, Ben Rea.

MOST EXPENSIVE CAT
A Californian Spangled Cat was bought for the record sum of $24,000 (£15,925) in January 1987.

MOST FAMOUS FELINE FALL
Patricia, a pregnant cat, was thrown into a river from the top of a bridge in Oregon, USA, by a vicious motorist in 1981. Two fishermen pulled Patricia from the freezing waters of the river. She lost her kittens but made a full rocovery.

TRAINING

The best way for your kitten to learn what it can and can't do is to establish behaviour rules and a routine right from the start. You should use your kitten's name when you are training it. It will start to recognise it the more you use it.

Wherever possible, feeding and grooming should be carried out at regular times of the day.

You should praise your kitten when it does something that you want it to. You could also give it something to eat or stroke it as a treat.

Your kitten may also need some 'negative' training. If you see it do something it shouldn't, say its name and say "No!" firmly.

Never hit your kitten or chase it away – it may think you are playing a game.

OUR KITTEN

LITTER TRAY TRAINING

Place the cat litter tray in a quiet, easily-reached spot.

Empty the litter tray every day wearing rubber gloves. Put the dirty litter in a plastic bag and throw it away. Refill the tray and put it on old newspapers.

You can tell when your kitten is about to go to the toilet. It will crouch down with its tail raised. If you see this, pick it up and take it quickly to its litter tray.

Put your kitten in its tray often, especially after it has finished eating. Leave your kitten to go to the toilet on its own.

Never rub your kitten's nose in it when he goes to the toilet in the wrong place. If you do, the kitten will be attracted by the scent and will regard that area as its permanent toilet. Indeed, always clean these areas thoroughly. You can buy special cleaners to get rid of the smell.

Most kittens will have learned how to use a tray from their mothers. Don't forget that cats are naturally clean animals so will adapt to using trays quite easily.

KITTEN'S DIET

Growing kittens have special dietary needs, just like humans. Kittens are carnivores, which means they eat meat to help them grow and make them strong. The keys to a kitten's diet are balance and variety. A balanced diet is made up of between 25-30% protein, 15-40% fat (more as your cat gets older) and up to 40% carbohydrates. Starchy foods are rich in carbohydrates and provide energy calories and bulk (fibre). Vegetables and fruit provide vitamins and bulk but should constitute no more than a third of the meal.

Water

Fresh water should be available all the time and changed two or three times a day. Your kitten will need more water if its diet is based on dry foods.

Manufactured Foods

These come in a range of forms: dried, soft-moist and tinned. They are ready to serve, easy to use and formulated to provide a balanced diet. But remember that a kitten has different nutritional needs to older cats, so look out for foods made especially for kittens.

Dried Food

This can be mixed with a gravy to provide extra ▶

water. You can make your own kitten gravy using boiling water, 1-2 teaspoons vegetable oil and ¼ stock cube.

Fresh Foods

It is a good idea to give your kitten at least one or two fresh meals a week if his diet is mostly tinned food.

Meat: beef, lamb or pork should be baked or grilled and then finely cubed or minced.

Poultry and Rabbit: feed your kitten cooked scraps but ensure there are no bones to choke on.

Fish: high in protein and can be given raw, cooked or from a tin.

Cheese: a very good source of protein.

Milk: a good source of protein and calcium but can cause an upset tummy.

TRUE STORY

Fallout

Abandoned cats are often reported to the RSPCA. However, in this case, not only had four kittens been abandoned but one of them was stuck high up in the branches of a very tall tree.

The kitten had been there overnight when the RSPCA received the call. By the time they reached the scene, the kitten was terrified and too scared to move. ▶

TRUE STORY: Fallout

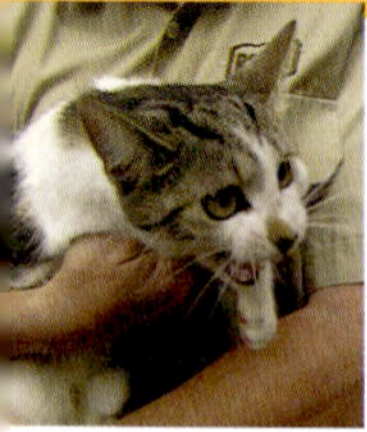

After trying to coax the kitten down, the RSPCA called the fire brigade, who needed a long ladder to reach the kitten.

However, just as the fireman reached the kitten, the kitten had a change of heart and climbed up even further to one of the branches at the very top of the tree.

The ladder now would not reach the kitten, so the firemen decided the best thing to do would be to cut down the branch so they could safely retrieve the cat.

Just at the last minute, things went wrong. The branch dropped off and the kitten went with it, tumbling down to the ground below.

Amazingly, the kitten landed and sprinted off. When the RSPCA managed to catch up with the poor kitten, they could see that he was very shocked, but apparently had no broken bones.

He was taken to Harmsworth for a thorough check-up. The vet checked the kitten all over and paid special attention to his mouth because it is quite common for kittens who have falls to fracture their palate or jaw.

The kitten was given the all-clear by the vet and was soon taken by the RSPCA to a special centre where he would wait to be rehomed. Let's hope the new owner doesn't live near any tall trees!

10

Show Names

Cat show names can be 26 letters long including the breeder's prefix. This is according to GCCF rules, the body which registers pedigree cats and kittens and organises shows. Here are our favourites:

1. Mouser Pawprint Bigwig
2. Twinklepaws Tiddles
3. Felix Foolish Fortuna
4. Gingertail Eric The Viking
5. Seablue Mini Cooper
6. Burlington Queenie Fay
7. Tell Tail Thomas
8. Ticklewhiskers Whitefoot III
9. Pussyfoot Golightly
10. Rumbletum Greedy Guts

IS MY KIT

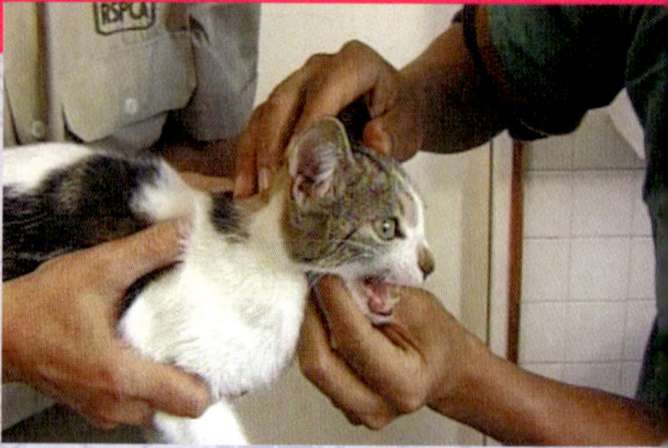

SIGNS OF HEALTH

A healthy kitten's eyes are clear and bright and its nostrils are clean and dry. It eats well and goes to the toilet regularly. A healthy kitten grooms itself regularly with its tongue and purrs when happy.

...handling by humans produces no signs of pain or discomfort. The kitten walks smoothly and does not limp or tremble.

SIGNS OF ILLNESS

The first signs of a kitten being unwell are often changes in behaviour. A sick kitten can become duller, more of a 'loner' or less active. Its appetite may either increase or decrease. It may start to look scruffy because a poorly kitten may not groom itself as much. The kitten may also meow more. If it is hurt, the kitten might cry out when the affected area is touched.

If you are worried about your kitten, call the vet for advice (see pages 56 and 57).

KITTENS IN THE W

Wild or 'feral' cats are the same species as the domestic cat. The difference is that they don't live with humans and have become wild.

Some are born into feral groups called colonies and others become feral or wild after being abandoned or getting lost.

Feral colonies can be found almost anywhere and there are likely to be more than one million such cats in the UK today.

The RSPCA thinks that feral colonies should be allowed to exist, as long as:

1. Someone takes responsibility for the cats and makes regular checks on their welfare. Wild cats are more likely to get sick or injured.

2. The owner of the site where the feral colony lives agrees to the presence of the animals.

If these conditions are met, the cats should be taken to the vet to be examined. Attempts should be

LD

ade to
ehome the
oung
ittens
r other
ats which
ren't totally
eral, as
hey deserve
he chance
o have a
aring owner.

ll other cats
which are too
vild to be
ehomed should
e neutered to
top the colony
om growing.

49

TRUE STORY

Sam'

Sam, a Persian cat, had his problem checked out by an RSPCA veterinary surgeon. A few months earlier, the cat's owner had brought Sam to the vet because he was sneezing.

The vet had given Sam a course of antibiotics to clear up a possible infection, but the sneezes stayed.

Three months later, Sam was still on antibiotics. He had a very runny nose so the vet decided to flush out his nose with salt water to check for any obstruction that might be causing the problem.

Nothing was found, so the vet had to give Sam an

Sneezes

naesthetic so she could x-ray Sam's chest to check
or signs of a different infection there. The vet and
urses were pleased to find that Sam didn't have any
ort of chest infection.

s they were bringing Sam out of the anaesthetic,
e cat suddenly stopped breathing.

e team had to work
ist. Sam had suffered
n allergic reaction to
e anaesthetic, which
 uncommon in cats.

ckily, their skills saved
am, and after a course
 different antibiotics,
s sneezes stopped
o. What a relief!

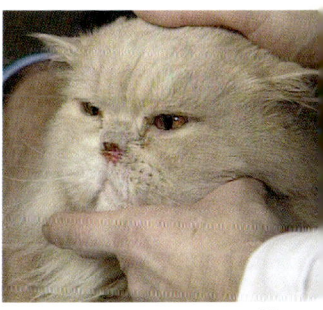

KITTEN AND PET

KITTENS LOVE

- PLANTS: THYME, CATNIP, SAGE, PARSLEY, CHICKWEED
- GAMES AND TOYS
- WARMTH
- SCRATCHING
- EXPLORING
- SLEEPING
- MARKING THEIR TERRITORY
- FOOD: CHEESE, YOGHURT, BONED FISH
- CLIMBING
- BEING STROKED BEHIND THE EARS AND UNDER THE CHIN

LOVES
HATES

KITTEN LOVE

KITTENS HATE

- ORANGE AND LEMON PEEL
- COLD
- BEING PICKED UP BY THE SCRUFF OF THE NECK
- TRAVELLING BY CAR
- GOING TO THE VET
- BATHS
- RAIN
- DOGS' TERRITORY
- LOUD NOISES, ESPECIALLY FIREWORKS
- THEIR FUR BEING STROKED THE WRONG WAY
- GETTING DIRTY
- BEING BLOWN ON
- THEIR TAILS BEING PULLED

ND **PET HATES**

WHEN TO C...

Everyone is ill from time to time, but it is more difficult to tell how serious an illness is with animals than humans. A visit to the vet costs an average of £10 to £20 and you might need to pay for medicine or treatment after that.

If you are worried about your kitten's health, you should keep it indoors so you can keep a proper eye on it. Sometimes rest, warmth and a little extra attention may be all your kitten needs.

There are certain signs, however, that you should not ignore.

If your kitten displays any of the following signs, check with an adult and talk to your vet immediately:
- Collapse
- Vomiting for more than 24 hours
- Diarrhoea for more than 24 hours
- Troubled breathing
- Bleeding

...L THE VET

Other common signs of illness:
- Sneezing, coughing or nasal discharge
- Over/undereating
- Increased thirst
- Drooling
- Meows of pain when touched
- Limping
- Constipation
- Frequent urination
- Discharge from, or severe scratching of, the ears.

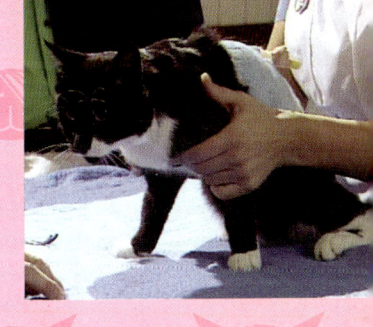

If you have to take your kitten to the vet, keep it warm and comfortable and take it in a carrier with its favourite blanket.

TRUE STORY — The Sn...

Top Cat was just under a year old when he was brought in to see the veterinary surgeon. His owner explained that he was called Top Cat because he always tried to climb to the top of everything and everyone, as the vet found out for herself!

Top Cat's owner explained the problem: Top Cat snored extremely loudly, not only when he was asleep, but even while he was awake.

Top Cat had to be anaesthetised before the vet could check down his throat to look for signs of anything that might be blocking Top Cat's airway.

The vet suspected Top Cat might have a growth called a polyp in his throat.

The vet's suspicions were correct. She could see immediately that Top Cat had an enormous growth in his throat. The vet was surprised he could breath at all.

ing Kitten

Surgery was needed to remove the polyp, which is a growth that starts off in the kitten's inner ear and, as it grows, gets lodged in the kitten's throat. Once awake, guess what! Top Cat was cured and his snores were gone for good.

KITTEN PART

Surprise your friends with a kitten-themed tea party!

Tuna Melt Crumpet Pizzas

(makes 4)

You will need:
- 1 small onion, chopped finely
- Knob of butter
- 4 crumpets
- 100g cheddar cheese, grated
- 2 teaspoons tomato puree
- 1 small tin dolphin-friendly tuna, drained
- Salt and pepper
- An adult to help

1. Heat the oil or butter in a pan, add the onion and fry for 3-4 minutes until soft. Add the tuna, heat through, then remove from heat.

2. Toast one side of the crumpets. Spread tomato paste on the untoasted side, cover with the onion and tuna mixture.

3. Sprinkle with grated cheese; season with salt and pepper before grilling the pizzas for 2-3 minutes until the cheese is bubbling. Serve.

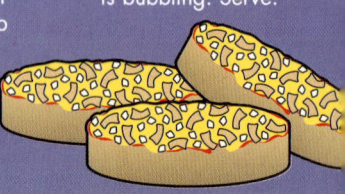

RECIPES

Sugar Mice (makes 4)

You will need:
- 170g icing sugar
- Half an egg white
- Few drops pink food colouring
- Few drops peppermint essence
- 8 milk chocolate chips
- 4 white chocolate drops
- 2 mint Matchmakers

1. Put the egg white in a bowl and whisk until frothy but not stiff.
2. Sift the icing sugar into a bowl.
3. Stir it into the beaten egg with a wooden spoon until the mixture is stiff.
4. Add a few drops of peppermint essence (according to taste) and a few drops of colour and knead into the mixture.
5. Break the mixture into four even-sized pieces.
6. Shape each piece into an oval and then pinch one end for a nose.
7. Add the chocolate chips for eyes and the chocolate drops (halved) for ears.
8. Cut the matchmakers in half to make the mouse tails.

Kittens spend a surprisingly high proportion of their time asleep. This is because, as hunters, they have adapted to using their energy in short bursts. As a result, kittens take great delight in rest and relaxation. Their love of comfort and warmth are important features of the feline lifestyle.

On average, kittens sleep for a total of 16 hours a day. 30% of this sleep is deep; 70% light.

As a hunter, even when your kitten is in its deepest sleep, it is still on 'stand-by' to defend its territory against intruders. While your kitten sleeps, its body is still receiving sensory messages so it can spring into action at the slightest hint of danger. When your kitten is taking one of its famous cat-naps, it will choose a vantage point where it is safe from attack.

SLEEP

If it is outdoors, this may be a sunny wall, roof or outhouse. In the home, where it feels more secure, your kitten may choose a chair, a bed or a warm place where it is quite hidden. Some kittens can be found in airing cupboards or curled up next to radiators in rooms that aren't used very often.

Cat and

- In the Middle Ages, the Christian church denounced cats as agents of evil. Superstitious people believed that witches could turn themselves into cats. As a result, cats were often burnt alive by Christians.

- The very first cat show was in 1598 but cat shows really began in 1871, with a large show, held at the Crystal Palace in London, for British Shorthair & Persian types.

- Originators of the cat-nap, cats sleep (in short bursts) more than any other mammal.

- Cats are more popular than dogs! According to the Pet Food Manufacturers Association, there are 7.7 million cats in the UK, compared to 6.6 million dogs.

- In ancient Egypt, killing a cat was a crime punishable by death.

- The ancient Egyptians even mummified cats and sometimes embalmed

Kitten Facts

mice were placed with them in their tombs.

- 92% of cats are 'Moggies' or non-pedigrees.

- The word 'cat' is 'gato' in Spanish, 'gatto' in Italian, 'neko' in Japanese, 'cath' in Welsh, 'kot' in Polish and 'ko-yang-i' in Korean.

- The British Government 'employs' more than 10,000 cats to keep official buildings rodent-free!

- When a cat licks you, notice how rough it feels. A cat's tongue is covered in tiny hooks or 'papillae'. They help the cat to lap up liquid and act as 'combs' to groom its fur.

- There are more than 500 million domestic cats around the world.

- Female cats, or queens, are pregnant for about nine weeks. When they give birth, their kittens are helpless. Their eyes remain closed for a week or more.

TRUE STORY

Up To

One day at the RSPCA's Animal Hospital, an owner brought in some kittens who needed serious help.

They weren't suffering from broken bones or a rare disease. In fact, they had fleas! Nonetheless, this was just as serious. The kittens were so badly infested that they were near to dying when the vet saw them.

Fleas are a common problem, but in this case the kittens were very young and the fleas were very many! They had sucked out a dangerously large quantity of the kittens' blood, leaving the kittens exhausted from scratching and weak from blood loss.

Because the kittens were so tiny, the owner was unable to treat the infestation safely without help. Fortunately, the hospital staff knew what to do.

They showed the owner how to groom the kittens with a special flea comb and they also recommended a

Scratch

special flea spray that was suitable for baby kittens. The owner would have to take great care when treating the kittens not to get any spray in their eyes, ears, nose and throat.

Had the owner tried to get rid of the flea infestation herself, she may have done more harm than good, as normal flea preparations sold in the shops (particularly powders) are not suitable for such young kittens.

PAWS a...

A domestic kitten uses its paws to explore things, just like humans use their hands. It uses its claws to dig into things, such as trees, so that it can climb them. A healthy, active kitten's claws are trimmed down automatically through play and exercise.

If it is kept indoors permanently, providing a scratching post or pad is important as it helps stop your kitten from attacking furniture and upholstery!

You can train your kitten to use the scratching post by gently lifting its paws up and down against the post. The posts can be easily made (see pages 70 and 71).

As your kitten scratches, it files its claws to keep them sharp. It is also a way of marking its territory,

CLAWS

because scent glands on the kitten's paws leave a smell where it scratches.

Kittens swing their paws out in front of each other as they walk, as if they are walking along a line. This is why they can walk along narrow ledges and fences. Fur between its toes helps a kitten to walk very quietly.

There are four toes on each of a kitten's front paws and one small toe slightly higher up its leg called a 'dew claw'. It is a bit like a thumb.

The claws are pulled in most of the time to stop them from being worn away too quickly and normally only come out during play or when they are needed for grasping and hunting.

MAKE IT! Scratch

Investing in a scratching post is often the best way to prevent furniture being shredded or scratched to pieces. Carpet-covered posts are often used. However, with very naughty kittens this may only encourage and confuse them into thinking that it is acceptable for them to claw your parents' best carpets! And that won't make either you or your kitten very popular! Natural fibres, like the rope used here, are better because man-made fibres are less hardwearing and more likely to cause your kitten problems if they become lodged in his throat.

YOU WILL NEED:
- An adult to help with the hammering and the glueing
- 2 large nails
- Strong glue
- Hammer

ng Post

- Sandpaper
- Two square planks of wood, same size (around 20cm x 20cm)
- Timber post approximately 40cm long
- Long piece of rope

1. Position the timber post in the centre of one of the squares of wood.
2. Nail one end of the post firmly in place.
3. Glue the rope tightly around the timber post until there aren't any gaps and the timber post is completely covered.
4. Allow to dry.
5. Place the other square plank of wood so that it lies flat on top of the post.
6. Nail the plank firmly in place, ensuring that the post is held firmly upright in position.

DON'T FORGET to sand down any sections of wood that are likely to give your kitten splinters.

FUR

Fur protects the kitten's skin and helps keep it warm. Kittens use their fur to signal to other kittens or to humans (see pages 82 to 85).

Kittens keep their fur clean by washing themselves. They do this by licking it with their rough tongues. Fur also keeps the kitten cool. When it is hot, many kittens wash to cool down, like having a shower.

Cats shed fur all the time. As old hairs fall out they are replaced by new ones. Their fur also grows thicker in winter for extra warmth. Kittens shed the extra fur in spring when the weather gets warmer.

GROOMING

When your kitten washes, it swallows loose fur. Sometimes it can get a fur ball stuck in its throat, which makes it sick. To help keep it healthy, you can brush your kitten's fur with special combs. Long-haired cats should be brushed daily whereas short-haired cats should be groomed once or twice a week, depending on the condition of their coat.

Long-haired kittens

Use a wide-toothed comb to remove dirt and tease out matts. Use a wire brush to remove all dead hair. Run a fine-toothed comb through the fur in an upward motion to help separate out the hairs and fluff it up.

Use a toothbrush to gently brush the shorter hairs on your kitten's face, avoiding the eye areas.

Short-haired kittens

Work down the kitten from head to tail with a fine-toothed metal comb. Use a soft natural bristle or rubber brush to comb along the lie of the coat.

Stroking your kitten between grooming sessions helps keep up the shine of its coat and keeps kitten happy!

ABOUT FUR

TRUE STORY

Up Or

Thrasher was a cat who had been stuck on a roof for three days! His owner was now very worried, so she called the RSPCA to see what they could do. The RSPCA officers agreed that it was a job for the fire brigade.

When the firemen arrived on the scene, they quickly got to work, having to negotiate a very tight alley between the houses with their long ladder. But they soon positioned the ladder so that one fireman could climb up and try to rescue the kitten.

The RSPCA officer showed the firemen how to use a special device to catch the kitten. It was now up to the fire brigade to safely rescue Thrasher.

As the kitten saw the fireman approach, he got scared and retreated behind a chimney stack, just out of the fireman's reach. Another fireman was needed to hold the first man's legs so that he could

The Roof

each over the top of the ladder and catch Thrasher.

Thrasher lived up to his name and was not going to make it easy for the fireman to bring him back down to the ground safely. A third fireman was called up the ladder to bring a bag. The firemen managed to put Thrasher in the bag and carry him down the ladder. Thrasher was safe at last.

Thrasher's owner was grateful and relieved. She explained how upsetting it had been to hear Thrasher's cries and not be able to help the cat.

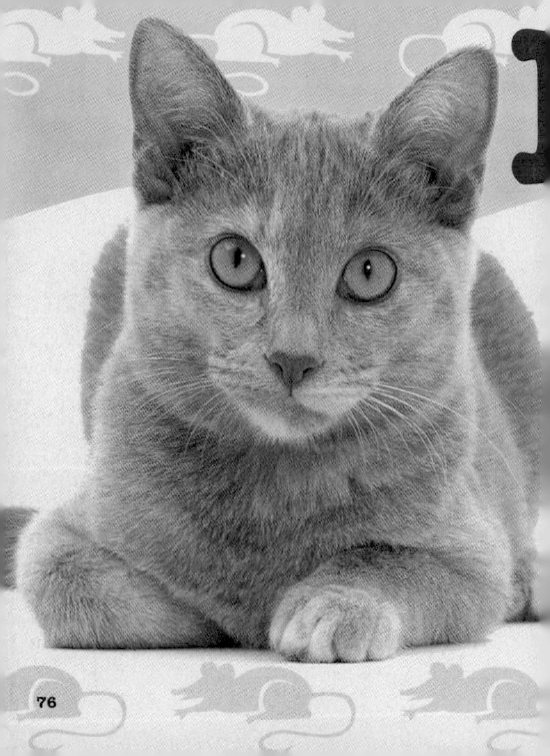

KITTEN TOYS

Kittens love to play and will play with almost anything. So be careful what you give them. Balls of wool or reels of cotton may provide a lot of fun for a kitten but can be dangerous. Here are some simple but safe toys you can give to your kitten.

1. Ping pong balls
2. Plastic pot or bottle (with lid) filled with rice
3. Squeaky rubber ball
4. Clockwork mouse
5. Catnip fish (see pages 78 and 79)
6. Plug with plug chain
7. Brown paper bag
8. Baby-safe small cuddly toy
9. Stuffed sock
10. Secure box with a marble inside

MAKE IT!

Catnip

Catnip, also known as catmint, is a plant that is popular with many cats and kittens. Kittens can smell catnip from the age of about six months. They enjoy chewing it and rubbing against it. Catnip may be bought at your local pet shop.

YOU WILL NEED:
- Square of thin paper
- Pins
- Needle and thread
- Scissors
- Felt-tip pen
- Dried catnip
- Pair of old, clean tights or stockings (ask first!)
- Square of coloured felt (approx. 30cm by 30cm)
- Pencil

Toy

1. Draw a fish shape on thin paper, making it about 10cm long and 5cm wide.
2. Pin the paper to the felt.
3. Carefully cut around the shape twice.
4. Pin the two pieces of felt together.
5. Sew around the edges using small stitches. Leave a big gap on the bottom edge for filling.
6. Push a wadge of tights into the fish. Try using a pencil to help push it into the corners if you need to.
7. Add the catnip, then more tights. Sew up the gap.
8. Draw on eyes with a felt-tip pen and squeeze the fish to make the smell come out more.
9. Ask an adult to check the stitching is really tight and firm before giving the toy to your cat.

CAUTION!!

Kittens' play is often tough! Keep an eye out for loose stitching which can cause problems if caught in a kitten's throat. Similarly, do not leave needles and thread lying about.

AS YOUR KITTEN GROWS

Development of kittens varies, but on average:

EYES
Change to permanent shade at 12 weeks.

TEETH
All milk teeth by eight weeks and permanent teeth appear at 12 to 22 weeks.

INDEPENDENCE
Earliest age a kitten can leave its mother is at eight weeks and not normally independent of mum until six months old.

VETERINARY ATTENTION
Spaying (females) at 12 weeks and neutering (males) at 26 weeks. A kitten should also be wormed regularly – ask your vet about this.

VACCINATIONS
First vaccination not until eight or nine weeks. Second vaccination at 12 weeks.

These vaccinations are against enteritis and cat flu and will need boosting every year. A kitten can also be vaccinated against the leukaemia virus. Don't allow your kitten outside until about a week after it has had its second vaccination or until your vet tells you.

DIET
Your kitten will need more food as it grows older and bigger.

HOW YOUR
TALKS T

Carefully watching your kitten's body language, particularly its tail and ears, is the key to understanding its feelings.

1. Tail curving gently upwards, ears may also be pointed forwards
= non-aggressive; kitten at rest.

2. Tail flush with back, raised at one end
= kitten is gathering information or exploring.

3. Tail tucked between legs
= defensive posture; kitten is planning an imminent escape.

4. Crouched down with tail pointed upwards
= kitten is about to go/is going to the toilet.

KITTEN
YOU

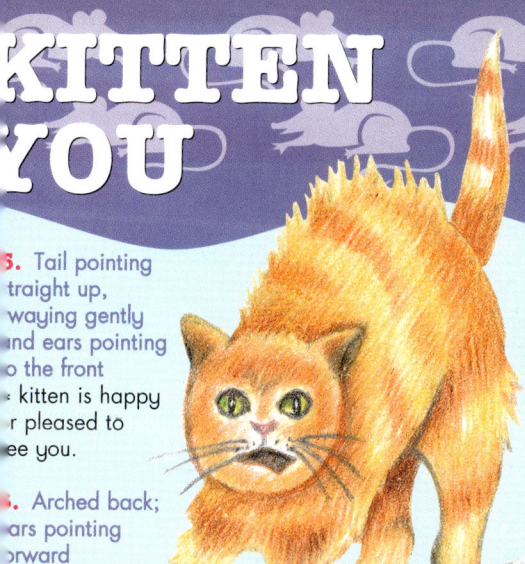

5. Tail pointing straight up, swaying gently and ears pointing to the front – kitten is happy or pleased to see you.

6. Arched back; ears pointing forward – saying hello. Kitten may also rub against you.

83

HOW YOUR KITTEN TALKS TO YOU

7. Kitten rolls over and shows you its stomach
= kitten showing trust and that it feels safe with you. It is unlikely to roll over like this if someone unfamiliar is nearby.

8. Tail twitching from side to side, ears pointing backwards
= aggression; kitten might attack or pounce. An angry cat may also spit or hiss and fluff up its fur to make itself look bigger. It may also put its claws out, showing it is ready to fight.

When playing, your kitten sometimes mixes signs that it is happy and angry. This is normal. For example, it may fluff up its fur and have its claws out but its ears pointing forwards.

Some kittens meow a lot to express how they feel. By using different meows, your kitten can tell you when it wants attention, is hungry, or wants to be let outside.

A happy kitten also makes a rumbling sound deep in its throat, called a purr. Stroking your kitten usually makes it purr.

Some kittens find other ways to talk to their owners. These tend to develop as the kitten grows and the bond between you strengthens. For example, a kitten may 'nuzzle' or rub you with its nose. Some kittens like to lick their owners' fingers or toes when showing their affection

House Moves

MOVING HOUSE

If you move to a new home, pack the following items together and make sure you can get to them easily:
- Litter tray
- Cat litter
- Food
- Cat bed and blanket
- Food and water dishes
- Toys

Your kitten will need these when you arrive.

A few days before you move, encourage your kitten to play in its carrier so it can get used to it.

When you are ready to leave, put a food treat inside the carrier and lift your kitten into it. Let your kitten use its litter tray before you put it into its carrier.

Don't put the kitten in the van with the furniture but take the carrier in the car with you.

On arrival at your new home, remember to shut all the doors before you open the pet carrier.

Let your kitten explore its new home and keep it inside for about a week until your kitten has settled in.

Give your kitten some food and water as soon as you arrive to endear it to its new home.

As soon as possible, put its bed and litter tra

and Holidays

in a suitable place and show them to your kitten.

Make sure your kitten is fitted with a collar and tag giving your new address and phone number before you let it outside.

HOLIDAYS

Some kittens like to travel but most prefer to stay at home where they feel safe.

If you are going on holiday and it is at all possible, ask a kind and responsible friend or neighbour to visit twice every day to feed your kitten and empty its tray.

If your kitten is old enough, your friend could also let it out for a while, then call it back in. If you have a cat flap, leave it unlocked so your kitten is free to go out when it likes.

Very young kittens do not like to be left alone, so it is best not to leave them alone overnight until they are about four months old and settled into your home.

Alternatively, when you go away, your kitten can stay in a special cat hotel or cattery.

Take your kitten's blanket to the cattery to remind it of home. All the other things should be provided.

We love
because

kittens they are...

- CUTE
- FUNNY
- WARM
- CUDDLY
- PLAYFUL
- NAUGHTY
- LOVING
- CLEVER
- BEAUTIFUL
- SOFT
- FLUFFY
- FURRY
- SKILFUL
- GRACEFUL
- FRIENDLY
- SMALL
- FAST
- FUN
- AFFECTIONATE

TRUE STORY

Tom's

When Tom was brought into hospital, he was very ill. His breathing was laboured and his owner thought Tom was dying.

The veterinary surgeon examined Tom and was extremely concerned. There was something very wrong with his tummy. She took an x-ray to confirm her suspicions of a ruptured diaphragm. Tom's organs were in a mix-up. It would take major surgery to put everything back in the right place and the vet thought that Tom had a 50-50 chance of recovery.

Tom was put in an oxygen tent before the operation. When surgery began, to the vet's horror, the hole in Tom's diaphragm was huge – much bigger than she had thought! Repairing the tear would take longer than she had expected.

As the minutes passed, Tom's chances of recovery were fading. Tom had been under anaesthetic for

Tum

over an hour, so the vet had to work fast.

Suddenly, at the end of the operation, Tom's heart stopped. The team had only minutes to get it beating again.

Their efforts were rewarded. Tom's heart started working again, but the vet was still not hopeful.

But Tom was a fighter. Just three days later, he was on his feet again. He had made amazing progress and Tom's owners were very lucky. They were told to keep him inside for at least two weeks and to give him lots of love and attention.

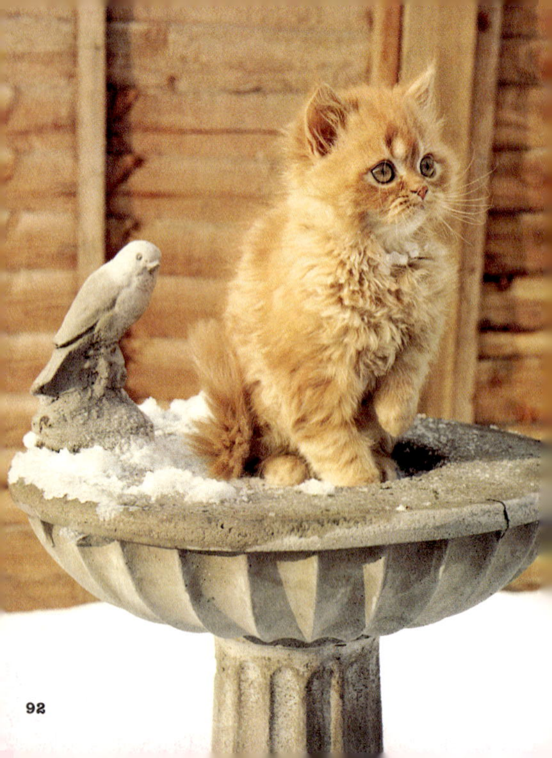

My kitten's name is

....

....

I got my kitten from

....

....

It was .... weeks old.

My kitten's birthday is

....

Describe your kitten's appearance:

....

....

....

Draw your kitten:

YOU AND YOUR KITTEN

My kitten's favourite food is

....
....
....

When my kitten is hungry, it tells me by

....
....
....

My kitten's favourite drink is

....
....
....

When my kitten is thirsty, it tells me by

....
....
....

My kitten's favourite toy is

....
....
....

My kitten's favourite game is

....
....
....

When my kitten is happy, it tells me by

....

....

When my kitten is scared, it tells me by

....

....

My kitten's favourite place to sleep is

....

....

My kitten's favourite person is

....

My kitten's favourite scratching place is

....

....

I love my kitten because

....

....

....

....

My kitten is cute because

....

....

....

Tips for

It is recommended that if you have any queries about a kitten's health or welfare you contact your local vet, the RSPCA, or one of its affiliated societies in Scotland or Ireland. The telephone numbers of these organisations are listed below, but the RSPCA can usually suggest a local body that they recommend.

Royal Society for the Prevention of Cruelty to Animals
Telephone:
(08705) 555999

Scottish Society for the Prevention of Cruelty to Animals
Telephone:
0131-339 0222

Ulster Society for the Prevention of Cruelty to Animal
Helpline:
(0990) 134329

MICROCHIP YOUR KIT!

If a kitten goes missing it is very distressing. You should ask your vet to microchip your kitten. The microchip contains a special number for just your kitten and can be painlessly inserted under the skin of your kitten. A central computer contains all ownership details under the special number and is 'read' by a scanner held by all local authorities, dog wardens, vets and RSPCA animal centres.

ts

97

Little Book of Kittens

Editor: **Jaynie Senior**
Writer/Researcher: **Sarah Armstrong-Prior**
Art Editor: **Paul Chamberlain**
Cover design: **Helmuth Rautenbach**

Illustrations: **Carol Pike**

Pictures on cover and pages 6, 14, 18, 22, 29, 36, 44, 49, 63, 72, 76, 80, 88, 97

supplied by **Bruce Coleman**